CHAKRAS

PLAIN & SIMPLE

CHAKRAS

PLAIN & SIMPLE

SASHA FENTON

THE ONLY BOOK YOU'LL EVER NEED

Cover design by Jim Warner
Interior design by Kathryn Sky-Peck
Hampton Roads Publishing Company, Inc.
Charlottesville, VA 22906
Distributed by Red Wheel/Weiser, LLC
www.redwheelweiser.com
Sign up for our newsletter and special offers by going to
www.redwheelweiser.com/newsletter/

*The author and publisher are not responsible for any adverse effects or consequences resulting from
the use of any practices, procedures, or preparations included herein.
Individuals should not use chakra healing methods as a replacement for treatment
from a medical professional.*

ISBN: 978-1-57174-773-0
Library of Congress Control Number: 2017935339
Printed in Canada
MAR
10 9 8 7 6 5 4 3 2 1

Contents

With grateful thanks to Lynne Lauren
who gave me some valuable information.

Part One

WHAT ARE CHAKRAS?

An Introduction to Chakras

1

The word chakra derives from the Sanskrit word *cakra*, which means "wheel" or "cycle." Chakras are variously described as spinning vortices, cones, discs, or even cogs. Imagine a length of pipe running through your body from head to toe, and along its length are seven cones that resemble the open ends of trombones, sticking out of the front and the back of the body. Now imagine that these cones are spinning. Each of these cones is an energy node, a swirling wheel where matter and consciousness meet. The invisible energy that moves within these cones is called *prana*, our vital life force, the metaphysical energy that keeps us healthy and alive.

These seven spinning cones are the chakras. They are located from the bottom of your spine (your tail bone) and ascend upward and out through the crown of your head. Each chakra spins in the direction opposite to the previous one.

You cannot see chakras on an X-ray or a scan because they are part of a "*subtle*" energy system, much the same way that your aura is an invisible emanation of your body's energy. The chakras link with the endocrine system, the nerve ganglia that lie along the spinal column, and also, therefore, with the glands that supply us with hormones such as adrenaline, insulin, estrogen, and progesterone.

Chakras are always active, as they are constantly monitoring things around such us as light, warmth, sound, smells, tastes, comfort, and discomfort. Chakras relate to the five senses of smell, taste, touch, hearing, and sight, as well as our senses of intuition and spirituality. The chakras sense and measure the surrounding elements and then balance our bodily interaction with

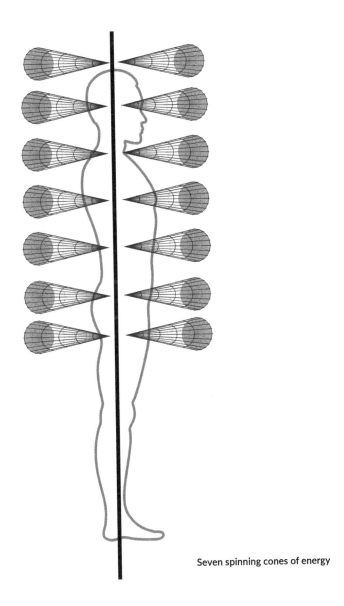

Seven spinning cones of energy

them. Chakras work with the human aura to let us know when we are getting too hot, cold, wet, or dry for comfort. They sense when the wind is too strong and perhaps when a rainstorm will come. They are part of the human survival system, and they act as an early warning system. Many cultures consider chakras to be a very ancient form of survival mechanism that exists in all animals and human beings. Chakras also help us to sense and calculate emotional atmospheres, so if a situation is likely to turn ugly, the chakras alert our sixth sense, to tell us to prepare for fight or flight.

When a chakra is closed, partially blocked, misaligned, or too open, it throws some part of our health, personality, or consciousness out of alignment. I know from my own experience that exhaustion and worry can make me lose perspective, and when this happens, problems that I can normally handle perfectly well suddenly appear overwhelming. When I am overtired or very worried, I forget to eat. When I start to eat again, I might overdo it, and my blood glucose can rise into unhealthy levels. In this situation, some energy healing directed into my solar plexus chakra works miracles, both on the physical and emotional level. In *Chakras Plain and Simple*, we will discuss the physical and emotional systems governed by each of the seven chakras.

There are three concepts inherent in the chakra system. These are:

- The physical body, which embraces health and strength, or sickness, weakness, and discomfort.

- The subtle or psychic body, which includes the mind, intellect, ego, and subtle feelings. This level helps us to "know" when something is wrong. (If you are a healer, this level is the one that helps you feel what is amiss within the bodies of those you are healing.)

- The spiritual world, which allows us to be psychic and mediumistic, to contact spiritual guides, to tap into people's past and future lives, and ultimately, to contact the Universe or the Divine.

A Brief History

The knowledge of the chakra system has its origins in ancient India, and it is incorporated into Hinduism, Jainism, and Buddhism. Chakras are mentioned in the Vedas, the four holy books that Hindus believe date back to before 2500 BC. The earliest mention of the chakras is in the later Upanishads, including Brahma Upanishad and Yoga Tattra Upanishad. This early Vedic model was later adapted into Tibetan Buddhism.

Sir John Woodroffe, who wrote under the name Arthur Avalon, translated two 16th century texts, the *Sat-Cakra-Nirupana* and the *Paduka Pancaka*, and published the translations in 1918 as his book titled *The Serpent Power*. The ideas in his book were complex. Later, the Theosophists took an interest in the book and the subject, and they removed some of the unnecessary complications. One of the Theosophists, C. W. Leadbeater, meditated on the subject and then wrote his own ideas down in a book called *The Chakras*, published in 1927. Modern Indian scholars who have studied Leadbeater's ideas are in broad agreement with him.

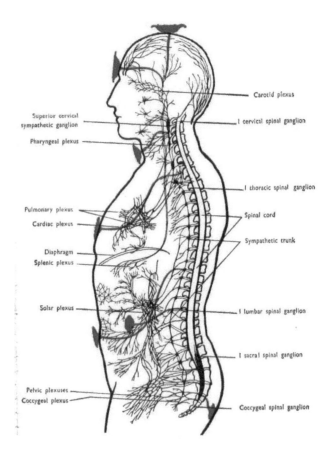

Carotid plexus

Superior cervical
sympathetic ganglion

I cervical spinal ganglion

Pharyngeal plexus

I thoracic spinal ganglion

Pulmonary plexus

Spinal cord

Cardiac plexus

Sympathetic trunk

Diaphragm
Splenic plexus

Solar plexus

I lumbar spinal ganglion

I sacral spinal ganglion

Pelvic plexuses
Coccygeal plexus

Coccygeal spinal ganglion

Chakra positions in relation to nervous system. This illustration is from the 1927 edition of *The Chakras* by C. W. Leadbeater. Here one can clearly see the conceptualization of the chakras as trumpet cones, into which and through which the prana, life force, flows.

In the Vedic (Hindu) tradition, the chakras are linked with Vishnu, who is "The Protector of the Universe." Vishnu is linked to the stars, the galaxies, and the universe, so those who have faith in astrology worship him.

Ancient Hindu tradition tells us that the soul is located in the solar plexus, heart, throat, brow, and crown chakras.

Other traditions use a similar system of connecting energy paths around the body, including the Chinese meridian system used in acupuncture, acupressure, and reflexology. There is even some similarity between the chakra system and the Kabala, and even with ideas contained in Islamic Sufism.

Vishnu

How Many Chakras Exist?

Not everybody agrees about the total number of chakras or all their locations, but here are some common theories:

- There are 78,000 chakras in the human body
- Seven are major chakras
- Twenty-one are minor chakras
- Forty-nine are tiny chakras
- The remainder are minute nano-chakras

Lotus Flower Symbols

Many Indian illustrations depict the chakras as lotus flowers (water lilies). The number of petals on each flower increases or changes with the growing complexity of each chakra. This doesn't match up with the idea of spinning cones and pipes, so the flower images are symbolic and give people a way to identify the chakras. Some people confuse these flowers with the chakras themselves, which irritates purists to the point that they reject the idea of the flower symbols completely! I am a great believer in doing what works for you, so if you wish to imagine the chakras as flowers, please do so. When I first learned about the chakras, my teacher described them to me as common flowers (poppies, marigolds and so forth) so I still remember them that way.

Sapta Chakra, from a Yoga manuscipt in Braj Bhasa lanaguage, 1899 [The British Library]. This illustration shows the seven major chakras as well as many of the minor chakras along the arms and legs.

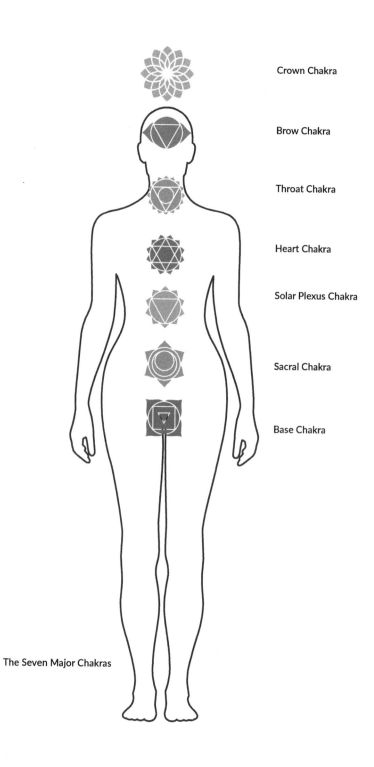

Crown Chakra

Brow Chakra

Throat Chakra

Heart Chakra

Solar Plexus Chakra

Sacral Chakra

Base Chakra

The Seven Major Chakras

The Seven Major Chakras

Let us return to our image of the pipe and the spinning cones. We can now discuss each of these seven energy "wheels" as the seven major chakras. Starting from the base of your spine, the seven chakras are

- The base (or root) chakra

- The sacral chakra

- The solar plexus chakra

- The heart chakra

- The throat chakra

- The brow (or third eye) chakra

- The crown chakra

The lower three chakras are associated with our most basic, fundamental needs, both physically and emotionally. They are sometimes called the *instinctual* chakras. The prana, or life force, is thought to vibrate more slowly through these chakras, and the energy is more dense.

The upper three chakras represent a more rapidly vibrating life force, and they correspond to our higher mental, emotional, and spiritual aspirations.

The heart chakra, between the higher and lower chakras, is known as the gateway chakra.

Chakras as Lotus Flowers

Using the Hindu lotus system, the seven chakras are described as follows:

Base: four petals

Sacral: six petals

Solar plexus: ten petals

Heart: twelve petals

Throat: sixteen petals

Brow: a petal on each side of a circle

Crown: one thousand petals

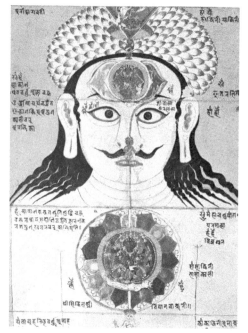

An illustration from an ancient manuscript shows the thousand-petalled lotus crown chakra, two-petalled brow chakra, and the sixteen-petalled throat chakra (Nepal, 17th century)

Chakra Colors

Each chakra is also associated with a color. These are:

Base: red

Sacral: orange

Solar plexus: yellow

Heart: green

Throat: blue

Brow: indigo

Crown: violet

Chakras and Astrology

Each of the chakras is associated with one of the seven planets that were known before the invention of telescopes. The signs with which they are linked belong to traditional astrology, predating the "new" planets of Uranus, Neptune, and Pluto.

Chakra	Zodiac Signs	Planet
Base	Aries, Scorpio	Mars
Sacral	Cancer	Moon
Solar plexus	Leo	Sun
Heart	Taurus, Libra	Venus
Throat	Gemini, Virgo	Mercury
Brow	Sagittarius, Pisces	Jupiter
Crown	Capricorn, Aquarius	Saturn

How to Work with the Chakras

2

The seven energy wheels, the chakras, keep our life force, prana, moving throughout our bodies. When this vital energy is blocked, the result is illness, both physical and emotional. In order to maintain health and vitality, it is necessary to understand what each chakra represents so we can focus our healing efforts on the proper chakra. We will go into the seven chakras in depth in part two of this book, but the following is a quick overview:

1. Base Chakra — Our foundation, our feeling of being grounded, our survival instinct

2. Sacral Chakra — Our ability to accept, and take pleasure in, other people and new experiences

3. Solar Plexus Chakra — Our self-worth, self-confidence, and self-esteem

4. Heart Chakra — Our ability to love and find inner peace

5. Throat Chakra — Our ability to communicate; self-expression

6. Brow Chakra — Our intuition, imagination, and wisdom

7. Crown Chakra — Our connection to spirituality

If a lower chakra is blocked, the upper ones can't work properly. A blockage in the sacral chakra might affect the actions of the throat or brow chakra, so you may discover that clearing one chakra helps others.

As you read through the chapters on each of the seven main chakras, you will come across character traits and emotional or psychological problems that you recognize within yourself.

Many health or emotional problems require conventional treatment, but complementary remedies can hasten the healing process. Thus, such things as gem therapy, color therapy, massage, reflexology, and spiritual healing can be of use. All of these can be directed toward specific conditions by identifying chakras that need to be cleared, balanced, aligned, mended, and healed.

The Basics:
Opening and Closing the Chakras

There are as many methods of opening and closing chakras as there are groups of channelers, healers, and other light workers. The following method comes from my friend, Barbara Ellen, and it uses common international flower images.

Opening the Chakras

Imagine yourself gathering light from the whole universe and then bringing this light down to the crown chakra. See the crown chakra as a purple lotus (water lily) and imagine it opening and allowing the light to enter through it. Then, allow the light to come down as far as the forehead chakra, at which point a large blue eye opens up. Allow the light to come down as far as the throat, at which point a pale blue cornflower opens up. Allow the light to come down to the heart chakra, where a bunch of green leaves opens up. Allow the light to come down to the spleen chakra and let a large yellow daisy or dahlia open up. Allow the light to come down to the solar plexus chakra, where a large orange marigold opens up. Allow the light to come down to the base chakra, where a big red poppy opens up. Then allow the light to filter down through the legs and to fill out the whole body and the surrounding aura. Finish by imagining the light extending down into the earth.

Closing the Chakras

Start by imagining the light that has reached down into the earth being turned off. Then turn off the light in your legs until you reach the base chakra. Now turn off the light there and carefully close down the red poppy. Next, turn off the light up to and beyond the solar plexus and close that flower down tightly. Continue the process until you have finished, and then send the light off into the universe.

Frankly, it is more important to learn how to close the chakras than to open them, because they open of their own volition as soon as you do any kind of psychic or spiritual work. They will also open if you talk about psychic matters, read about them, or when you watch a psychic or spooky television program. Chakras that have been left open can lead to bad dreams, feelings of psychic invasion, and other uncomfortable sensations.

Some people like to open their chakras from the bottom upwards, so if that is your preferred method, that's fine.

Clearing the Chakras

This idea comes from Eve Bingham. Imagine crystal clear water entering your crown chakra and running through your body and out through your fingertips and toes. Focus on giving each chakra a good wash. When you have finished, close your chakras carefully, using the method previously described.

If you feel that something has really upset you, as soon as you can get around to it, take a shower. While you are under the shower, wash your hair thoroughly, and don't forget to give the underneath of your feet a good wash. Then go through the chakra closing procedure again. This can actually help if someone upsets you, because the nastiness will have got into your aura or subtle body and got stuck there like bits of Velcro. A bath will help, but a shower does a better job of washing unwanted subtle material away from the body.

Strengthening Weak Chakras

Each of the seven main chakras rules a different portion of a person's psychology and character. We all naturally have one or two chakras that are stronger than the others. Or we might even have one chakra that is performing very badly. We can strengthen our weaker chakras in various ways:

- We can work on our psychology by trying to think, behave, or react in a way that is less harmful to ourselves and to others, but this is only practical if the emotional or psychological problem is fairly mild. Also, it is not always easy to change oneself.

- Hypnotherapy or emotional freedom technique (EFT) might be useful.

- You can ask a healer to channel light and strength into your weaker chakras.

- You can take advantage of healing techniques such as crystal therapy, color therapy, and aromatherapy. I suggest relevant crystals, colors, and essences for each chakra later in this book.

- Reflexology, acupuncture, and acupressure all work on the meridian lines, which themselves align to the chakras.

- You can do a certain amount of self-healing with these techniques.

- Those of you who are into pagan ways may wish to use items that connect to certain chakras on an altar.

The chakras are associated with specific body parts and with specific ailments, so healers can work directly on the right chakra for each ailment. For instance, you would work on the sacral and base chakras for bowel problems.

Keeping Yourself Grounded

All psychic work can make the practitioner or the recipient feel light-headed and "spacey." If this happens to you, take your shoes off and walk around on the ground, or even lie down on the ground for a while, if possible. As soon as you can do so, go out of doors and stand on the grass or the earth for a few minutes. This will act like the earth wire or a lightning conductor, and it will ground you once again.

If you get a headache while giving or receiving healing or any other kind of psychic work, stop for a while. The headache denotes too much activity going on in your upper chakras, and a need to ground and balance the lower ones. It might be worth focusing on sending light from your body downward through the earth at this time. Another idea might be to lick a little salt or to hold a couple of crystals in your hands, as these items are part of the earth realm.

Always close your chakras down after working. If you haven't the time to do a proper close down, or if you forget how to do it, use this simple trick: Imagine yourself in a purple sleeping bag, zipped up all around you, and even over your head. That will strengthen your aura.

Meditation and Psychic Work

Your meditations will be more effective if you open your chakras first. Don't forget to close them down again when you have finished. The chakras will open easily as soon as you give healing to others or perform any channeling or any other kind of spiritual or psychic work. Do remember to close them down afterward.

Part Two

THE
SEVEN
CHAKRAS

The
Base
Chakra

3

Vedic name:	Muladhara
Number:	The first chakra
Other names:	Root chakra, red chakra
Central concept:	Survival, life
Color:	Red
Lotus petals:	Four
Shapes:	Square
Element:	Earth
Planet:	Mars
Zodiac sign:	Scorpio
Health connection:	Legs, base of the body
Balance:	Yang, masculine, positive
Gland:	Adrenal
Sense:	Smell
Mantra:	Lam
Music:	Drumming

Location

The base chakra is located at the base of the spine and it goes through the body at the bottom of the trunk. Some say that its sphere of influence includes the hips and thighs, while others say that it includes the whole of the legs and feet, linking the body to the earth via the feet.

Basic Purpose

The base chakra symbolizes the drive for survival. It is the first of the *instinctual* chakras, as opposed to emotional, mental, or spiritual chakras. The base chakra rules such things as the ability to sense danger and to seek safety by taking cover. It also relates to the basis of anything, such as the home from which one ventures out into the world, the mother, one's family history, family honor, the past, the collective unconscious, and even the earth itself.

The realm that is ruled by the base chakra and that of the sacral chakra, which is the next one up, overlap a little, because both rule parts of the lower trunk, but their attitudes are different from each other. The base chakra is masculine, yang, and active, while the moody sacral chakra is feminine, yin, and more likely to react to situations than to create them. The sexual image of the base chakra is the act of making love, or even of energetic sex, whereas the sacral chakra is more involved with the results of making love—pregnancy.

A Strong Base Chakra

After about six weeks, a baby will begin to look around. It will smile at its mother, and it will recognize and respond to the faces and voices of its family members, but those first crucial six weeks are all about *survival*. An infant needs food, warmth, and protection. It doesn't need an impressive lifestyle or celebrity parents, it needs love and the assurance that it will not be abandoned or uncared for. The base chakra has a similar outlook, as its central concern is self-preservation. There are other topics associated with this chakra, but its main concern is the business of keeping its owner alive and in one piece.

This is the most down to earth and practical of the chakras, because without its influence, we wouldn't have the sense to come in out of the cold or to eat properly. The base chakra gives us our awareness of the world around us and our place on earth and in society. It rules the need for practical security, including such things as finding a safe area in which to live, obtaining the necessities of life, and making a reasonable lifestyle for ourselves. If danger threatens, the adrenaline associated with this chakra kicks in and gives us the instinct for fight or flight.

This chakra represents the basis of life and the background that shapes us, and it refers to the kind of family we had and the atmosphere that was around us when we were young. It relates to childhood experiences that affect us many years later.

A friend once told me that when she was a little girl, her father often had affairs with other women, which naturally made her mother extremely unhappy and angry. Whenever the father snuck off to spend a night with his latest fling, her mother would vent her rage and frustration on my friend. The sheer terror of coping with an out-of-control mother who was lashing out for some undisclosed and incomprehensible reason was so dreadful, that in later life, my friend subconsciously married a man whose main virtue was that he was unlikely to stray—unfortunately his *only* virtue.

Those with a healthy base chakra are blessed with common sense, a love of the earth and of nature—so powerful base chakra folk might be talented gardeners, carpenters, builders, farmers, or civil or mechanical engineers. These subjects are unlikely to be stupid where money and possessions are concerned. They can be assertive, confident and courageous, strong willed and capable, able to initiate things and to take calculated risks. Base chakra individuals can find a way of making something that the world will buy, and then go on to build an enterprise and make a great deal of money out of it. They are the workers of the world and they won't allow others to provide for them or for their families unless absolute disaster occurs and, even then, only until they can get back on their feet. The base chakra is linked to one's choice of profession due to the need to survive in a financial and practical sense.

On a lighter note, this chakra relates to rhythmic music, dance, and to the joy of moving to music. The rhythm, movement, and pleasure that we get from playing sports also belong to this chakra. Much the same goes for the pleasure that we get from making love.

Too Much Base Chakra

These people can have some good qualities and they can earn respect and admiration from others, but they are not easy to live or work with. Some are nice enough, but they are so wrapped up in their work or in making money that they have little time for the niceties of life or for spirituality.

In extreme cases, they develop troublesome qualities such as addictions to alcohol or sex, and some sufferers display obsessive and compulsive behavior. At the very worst end of the spectrum, these people can't be bothered to understand others or to care about them. They can be selfish and materialistic, greedy, angry, cruel, racist, bigoted, bitchy, and nasty. This may be linked to a very low level of self-esteem and some deep-seated fear, or it can be due to jealousy or an inability to see clearly through a fog of illusion and paranoia. Addiction to drugs or alcohol could even be at the back of this kind of behavior.

Not Enough Base Chakra

Those who have a weak base chakra might live "in their heads" so that they lack practical, earthy realism. They might be full of self-pity, or they may be weak and frightened. They may be unable to supply themselves with the basic needs in life, and while they have good intentions, they might never quite get around to doing anything. At worst, these subjects are filled with neurosis, anxiety, tension, and terror with no healthy outlet for their fears.

One simple way to add courage is to wear something red. This lifts the spirits and increases courage.

Body and Health

Needless to say, the ailments associated with the base chakra are those associated with the base of the body. Ailments include cervical erosion, thrush, cystitis, venereal diseases, piles, anal fistulas, prostate problems, testicular problems, sterility, impotence, ejaculation problems, vasectomy, incontinence, vaginal problems, AIDS, constipation, diarrhea, and much else about the human "plumbing" system that we don't talk about in polite society.

There may also be problems associated with the hips, legs, and feet, including sciatica or the circulation of blood through the limbs. This chakra may also be linked to high blood pressure levels, arthritis, and possibly also to some forms of cancer. Along with several other chakras, the base chakra can relate to such eating disorders as anorexia, bulimia, and overeating as part of a mix up of the survival mechanism with the predisposition to addictive behavior.

This chakra is also said to represent the skeletal system, including the teeth. Its connection to the sense of smell means that the nose is included.

According to some legends, if a person has a problem with the left hip, leg, or foot, he or she has problems with the mother. If the right side is giving problems, the child/father relationship was difficult.

If you want to heal base chakra problems, you may also wear pink rather than the traditional red, as pink is gentle and effective, where red may feel angry, hot, and rushed.

Spiritual Link

The image related to this chakra is of conception and the start of life, so this chakra symbolizes the starting point of the kundalini journey and the commencement of the search for spirituality. Interestingly, despite this being the most basic and earthy chakra, it is where the search for the connection to the divine begins.

Problems might arise because the subject has a particularly rigid attitude to religion, choosing to become part of a world where everything normal is forbidden. This is the realm of self-appointed gurus who enjoy telling others how to live. A healthier form of religious rigidity includes silent orders of monks and nuns. These people give up normal life to focus on serving God, and while we have great respect for them, we all know that this lifestyle is by no means natural, because if we all suddenly took to living in a locked down convent, the human race wouldn't be able to reproduce itself, and thus it would die off. In one way, belonging to a religious institution is rather like being in the army, because those involved don't have to worry about providing for themselves or their families. Their basic needs of food, warmth, clothing, and shelter are met. And so, by this circular route, we are back to square one, which is that the base chakra rules the instinct for survival and basic human needs.

Exercises for the Base Chakra

Affirmation: I AM

This exercise can be done anywhere, but is best done outside, so that you are in contact with the earth.

- Sit cross-legged with your back erect. Feel the base of your spine—your tailbone—make contact with the ground.

- Close your eyes and take a few deep breaths.

- Now visualize your root chakra as a glowing red ball. Breathe in and allow this ball of energy to increase in strength with each breath. Feel its warmth grow and expand inside you.

- Visualize this red ball of energy as a rose or poppy, its roots growing down deep into the earth, grounding you.

- With each breath in and out, this bloom begins to open, drawing up the life force from the earth. Cherish its beauty and energy as it opens within you.

The
Sacral
Chakra

4

Vedic name:	Svadhistana
Number:	The second chakra
Other names:	Spleen chakra, orange chakra
Central concept:	Creation, emotions
Color:	Orange
Lotus petals:	Six
Shapes:	Crescent moon, pyramid
Element:	Water
Planet:	Moon
Zodiac sign:	Cancer
Health connection:	Ovaries, testes
Balance:	Yin, feminine, negative
Gland:	Ovaries, testes
Sense:	Taste
Mantra:	Vam
Music:	Strings

Location

The sacral chakra is located in the middle of the abdomen below the navel. It links with the lumbar spine, the sciatic nerve, and the sacral plexus. The Latin name for this chakra is *genitalia*, which corresponds with the Vedic connection to the ovaries and testes.

Basic Purpose

The sacral chakra is the second of the *instinctual* chakras, as opposed to the mental or spiritual chakras, so it works on an instinctive and intuitive "gut" level but unlike the more basic nature of the base chakra, the sacral chakra taps into the emotions. This chakra concerns sharing but it also rules independence. The ideal situation is to share with others but not to lean on them or drain them or in turn, to be drained by others. This chakra rules feelings, emotions, and moods, along with appetites and the desire for sex. However, while base chakra is aggressively masculine and active, the moody sacral chakra is feminine, and the receptive, passive, feminine aspect of this chakra makes it more likely to *react* to situations than to *create* them.

A Strong Sacral Chakra

The sacral chakra is the largest of all the chakras and it is the seat of the emotions, so it is not surprising that so many people get queasiness in the tummy when they become nervous or excited. Some people get the urge to run to the bathroom before something they find nerve-wracking, such as performing on the stage.

This chakra connects with a woman's womb, ovaries, and menstrual cycle, so it is associated with mood swings and temperament. The Hindu name, *Svadhistana*, derives from the Sanskrit, as do the ancient forms of Greek and ancient Hebrew, and the word that has come down to us via all these languages is *hysteria*! The ancient Greek name for the womb was *hystera*, and the ancient Greeks believed that a woman became hysterical as a direct consequence of a malfunctioning womb! It is true that the pain and discomfort in the womb can make a woman short tempered and depressed, but it is crazy to attribute all feminine unhappiness to an ailing womb. People of both sexes who suffer back pain, neuralgia, or rheumatism can be touchy and bad tempered.

The sacral chakra is linked astrologically to the moon. Ancient sky watchers considered the moon restless and temperamental due to its habit of changing shape and disappearing altogether for days on end. The cycles of the moon have always been linked to the female cycle, and the moon is metaphorically linked to the feminine concepts of intuition, feelings, and hunches. This chakra is too low on the chakra scale to allow for logic or intellect, but it is the source for "gut feeling" knowledge.

One very important facet of the sacral chakra is that those who have strong sacral chakras know what's best for themselves. They also know when something or somebody is harmful to them. For instance, someone with a strong sacral chakra will suspect that something is wrong inside his body long before anything shows up medically. It can also help a person to see or feel that something is wrong with a loved one.

Those who have a strong sacral chakra are able to set boundaries, so they are unlikely to be pushed around, or to be frightened by others or treated as a victim. They set sensible rules for their children to follow and they are consistent, so their children know where they stand from one day to the next. These subjects won't make unrealistic sacrifices for others, and they don't become martyrs, so they are pretty content with their environment. They appreciate the good things that they have and they don't complain about what they lack. They focus on what's good in their lives rather than worrying about the things they don't have. They set boundaries for their own behavior. They are pleasant neighbors, good friends, and welcome relatives, who get on with most people and make the best of most situations. Their self-esteem is healthy but it is not over the top.

This chakra rules sexual attraction and the pleasure one gets from sex. The sacral chakra is associated with creativity; one form of creativity is the creation of new life, therefore, this chakra rules the desire for children and the desire for a happy family. While we all know that sex can be a solitary pleasure or even a group experience, the reality is that lovemaking is best enjoyed as part of a twosome. It is one of the few things that can be given away to a lover and enjoyed by oneself at the same time. A lovely meal is a similar thing because it is so much nicer when shared.

As with the base chakra, the sacral chakra connects the person to the past, the family background, the collective unconscious, and the roots. The past can influence people in many ways, but someone with a healthy sacral chakra isn't too badly influenced by a bad start in life. This subject develops enough awareness and strength of character to cherry-pick the good things from his past and to turn away from the legacy of the bad ones. These people can choose to allow the past to influence them or they can choose to forget it. For instance, these subjects may choose to run their home and family life in exactly the same way that their parents did, or they may decide to take a very different route. These people may feel that their past experiences, background, and roots are pretty good, and they probably feel proud of these things.

Those who have a strong sacral chakra are not in love with money but they appreciate the freedom that it confers. These folk can succeed in a job or in business by creating goods that people want to buy, and they take pleasure from the creative process of building a business. Their intuitive understanding of other people makes them excellent employers and fine salespeople. They are sociable and somewhat ambitious, although not necessarily money-minded. They work well in collective situations where harmony and pulling together are needed. This chakra endows the individual with imagination and intuition, along with a sincere nature and an ability to empathize with others. Needless to say, these people make excellent counselors, healers, nurses, psychic readers, and friends. The motherly nature of this chakra can lead these subjects to create or gather a large family around them or to care for young people on a professional basis.

Vedic tradition suggests that those who have strong sacral chakras come into this world knowing that they will never drown or be harmed by water. I guess someone with a strong sacral chakra would be a successful sailor, swimming pool attendant, or fishing boat worker!

Too Much Sacral Chakra

When there is too much emphasis on the sacral chakra, cravings and desires can run wild, leading to overeating or becoming addicted to such things as chocolate, alcohol, or prescription drugs. There may be an addiction to appalling relationships. When I worked as an astrologer, I used to come across clients who wanted their lives to be as full of drama and excitement as the soap operas that they watched on television, so they would go into relationships that promised this. Their worries inevitably revolved around sex, infidelity, abandonment, and love.

Taken to the extreme, jealousy, manipulation, and violent outbursts can rule the day, as can excess of all kinds—even choosing to have more children than the person can cope with.

Not Enough Sacral Chakra

In some cases, there is a kind of choice going on here, which is not so much a personality problem as such, but a lifestyle choice that leads the person away from loving or sexual relationships. For example, there are some who prefer to put their energies into work rather than family life, and while this is not necessarily a bad thing, it does make for a one-sided lifestyle if work is all there is. We have all read about tycoons who spend so much time at work that they either don't have partners, or if they do marry, sooner or later their partners wander off and find someone who's actually around and who shows some interest in them. Some relate well to animals, which shows they have loving natures but not necessarily directed at other human beings.

In severe cases, those who have a very weak sacral chakra are timid, withdrawn, and nervous. They may be frightened of getting involved with others because they lack romance or real emotion. They find it hard to understand or empathize with other people. They may become victims or martyrs when in relationships.

When I gave readings, I would often come across a self-sufficient woman who was happy to be on her own. Often, she had done her bit with regard to marriage and children, and she was now happy to pursue her interests and even to have a partner or two—but without having to wash their underwear. These women were into gardening, music, sports, pets, bingo, and many other things—they were perfectly happy on their own.

Sometimes a person with a weak sacral chakra can be so busy doing things for others that they put their own needs last, so that they end up feeling as though they have lost themselves.

Body and Health

The sacral chakra rules the organs of procreation, thus the uterus, ovaries, fallopian tubes in women, and the testes in men. Problems related to fertility come under this chakra. Many ailments here are similar to those of the base chakra, so we might find problems related to the womb, ovaries, and fallopian tubes, and also the bowels. This chakra also rules impotence, prostate problems, and sexual dysfunction, and it rules such things as fibroids and ovarian cysts. This area rules lower back pain, slipped discs, sciatica, and pain in the long muscles of the lower back, along with movement and walking that are affected by lower back conditions.

This chakra rules nourishment, so it relates to eating disorders, including over-eating, anorexia, and bulimia. Allergic conditions, migraine, and *Candida albicans* can be found here, as well as asthma and eczema. There is often a link with depression and dissatisfaction with life.

Spiritual Link

Whereas the base chakra rules the moment of conception, the sacral chakra represents the early stages of growth. The person searches for spirituality but doesn't yet know which direction this quest will take. This chakra is linked with feelings and intuition, so it will trigger unsettled feelings that warn us when something is wrong. On a less dramatic level, it is common for people to think of someone, only for that person to contact them later that day.

Some psychics say that this is by far the largest chakra, so if you want to strengthen your intuitive or psychic abilities, and don't have the time to go through the process of opening and closing all the chakras, open just this one. Do remember to close it down afterward, though.

Exercises for the Sacral Chakra

Affirmation: I Feel

- Do exercises that strengthen your lower abdomen, such as sit-ups and planks.

- Practice belly breathing. Make sure each inhalation fills your belly, not your chest.

- Tradition says that emotional or physical problems related to this chakra can be treated with a warm scented bath.

- Dance! One of the best ways of strengthening and opening this chakra is let your hips go, and feel the rhythms of the universe.

The Solar Plexus Chakra 5

Vedic name:	Manipura
Number:	The third chakra
Other names:	Yellow chakra, naval chakra
Central concept:	Energy, control, and belief
Color:	Yellow
Lotus petals:	Ten
Shapes:	Circle
Element:	Fire
Planet:	Sun
Zodiac sign:	Leo
Health connection:	Digestion
Balance:	Yang, masculine, positive
Gland:	Pancreas, endocrine
Sense:	Sight
Mantra:	Ram
Music:	Reed and horn music

Location

This chakra is located just above the naval.

Basic Purpose

The solar plexus chakra is associated with the ability to achieve one's aims and ambitions, thus it is linked to courage and self-confidence. It rules curiosity, the desire to acquire knowledge or to obtain the right kind of experience. Issues surrounding control and freedom can be found here. On one hand, this chakra symbolizes the self-control and the latitude that a person allows *himself*, but it can also relate to the ability to direct and control others.

A successful person has a definite purpose in life and a fair chance of achieving his or her aims. Combine this with comfortable relationships, good friendships, good health, an active mind, interesting pastimes, and the ability to have a good laugh from time to time, and we have the definition of a perfectly happy person. This chakra rules the *prana* or life force, and its allied concept of happiness. Naturally, the best relationship is the one we have with ourselves, so this chakra is about self-acceptance and self-worth, rather than self-consciousness or of being one's own worst critic.

A Strong Solar Plexus Chakra

The solar plexus chakra is the first of the *emotional* chakras rather than being one that is instinctive, mental, or spiritual.

When the sunny solar plexus chakra is working properly, it allows an individual to be happy and successful. It endows the subject with energy, willpower, and "get up and go." These lucky people have the confidence and courage to tackle new projects and the ability to see them through. They are alert and open to new initiatives and ideas, and they have the endurance to finish what they start.

These folk know their own strength, they don't get into fights and arguments for the sake of it, but they can stand up for themselves when necessary. They have leadership qualities, but they are neither domineering nor aggressive. They can choose to make sacrifices for loved ones on occasion but they won't allow themselves to become martyrs or victims.

The connection between the solar plexus chakra and the ability to study makes these folk good students and good teachers. The current emphasis on data and information suits these subjects, because these people absorb any amount of data. They become walking encyclopedias, but they need to guard against becoming know-it-alls or bores.

Money is important to these folk, but seeing themselves as successful and commanding the respect and admiration of others is their stronger motive. Whether their area of operation is business or whether their ambitions might point them in other directions, they will be keen to excel in something. Knowledge can be seen as power, and at the least, it can prevent others from walking all over them when it comes to negotiating. Someone with a fully functioning solar plexus chakra will make sure he or she is equipped with all the necessary information before walking into a difficult situation. These people are grounded, secure, and comfortable within the arenas in which they operate. They are decisive, capable, and intelligent, with a healthy sense of self-worth and a very good sense of humor. They don't go through life fearing illness or death, and they seldom fall ill.

The downside, even when the chakra is relatively well balanced, is that these subjects can make a mess of relationships. Loving relationships are not about winning or taking first place, or even about being the most exciting, richest, and most charismatic person around. They are about love and respect for the partner, along with give and take. These workaholic, persistent, persnickety, successful subjects may shine in the wider world, but they don't always make a success of relationships.

Too Much Solar Plexus Chakra

These subjects can be cold, logical, and analytical and they may use logical arguments in order to demolish the opinions of others. They make admirable computer programmers or analysts, because a computer doesn't have emotions. They abuse power, either by being argumentative, loud, and physical or by being cold and calculating.

At the very worst end of the spectrum, those who have an overabundance of solar plexus chakra energy are arrogant, domineering, angry, and irritable. They may be domineering or power hungry. They can be hurtful and sarcastic, and they may not hold back from attacking others physically, either. Alternatively, they can be fussy perfectionists who like to impose their obsessive standards on others while allowing themselves plenty of leeway.

They can be witty and amusing at times but it is unpleasant to be around them for too long. Yet they fear being alone, and therefore they find ways of binding others to them.

Not Enough Solar Plexus Chakra

Some people fall behind in the career success stakes due to increasing age or because they spend so much time at home with small children. Sometimes staying at home turns the mind to mush, so if these folk want to improve the action of their solar plexus chakras, they should take classes, learn a sport, or take dancing lessons. They should do puzzles, jigsaws, and crosswords; read books; and, if possible, get out and interact with others. This chakra is about curiosity, wit, humor, and awareness, so anything that increases the mental faculties will build up a weak solar plexus chakra.

In the worst case scenario, these individuals can be too flexible for their own good. They are people pleasers who lack the courage to negotiate for their own rights and requirements. They lack the confidence, intelligence, energy (and luck) that would help them to make a success of a project. A lethal cocktail of poor self-esteem, fear of risk, and a shortage of verve hold these folk back. They attract the attention of bullies, and they can be pessimists and losers. They might be apathetic and inert, they may lack intelligence, and they certainly lack passion. These individuals find it hard to make decisions, so they can jump into making the wrong choices, sometimes out of fear or even in a fit of pique. They are too self-effacing. Some can be successful on a superficial level, but they gain advantage by being slippery and treacherous, and they may delude themselves about their worth and their abilities.

Body and Health

Can you stomach it? Well, if you can't, the chances are that your solar plexus chakra is in trouble. This may be a temporary problem such as a stomach upset. The solar plexus chakra rules the digestive organs: the stomach, liver, pancreas, and gallbladder. There will be difficulty in converting food into energy, perhaps due to stomach ulcers, liver problems, gallstones, diabetes, or hypoglycemia. One result of this situation is fatigue. This person may gain or lose too much weight. This chakra is associated with the outer adrenal glands and adrenal cortex.

In some countries, there are parasites that enter the body through the skin or by other means, living in their host until they have completed part of their breeding or growing cycle; therefore, malaria, and bilharzia are associated with this chakra. The solar plexus chakra rules the skin and the sense of sight, so it is allied to the eyes.

Spiritual Link

Individuals who have strong solar plexus chakras know their own strength, and they tend to use it for the benefit of others. They don't pull others down or compete with them because this doesn't give them pleasure. On the contrary, they obtain pleasure by helping others reach their potential. This person's happiness, wit, and humor can be used to bring fun and joy to others. These subjects make excellent parents, and some of them choose to look after other people's children and to help youngsters develop skills and confidence. These individuals can encourage others to gain vision and clarity and make the best of themselves. Such people can be the bridge between the day-to-day world of material success on the one hand, and the need to pray and thank the Divine for help on the other.

Exercises for the Solar Plexus Chakra

Affirmation: I Act with Courage and Confidence

Ancient tradition suggests that people with a strong solar plexus chakra have the ability to travel astrally. If you want to try this, do the following:

- Start by relaxing on your bed, on your back.

- As you start to become sleepy, imagine yourself leaving your body, rising up, and traveling away for a while.

- Visualize a golden cord extending from your navel so that you can bring yourself back into your body.

The solar plexus chakra is associated with the sun, and being out in natural sunlight is a simple and powerful exercise.

- Practice yoga outdoors on sunny days.

- Sunbathing will help open your solar plexus chakra. Lie on your back, feel the sun's warmth on your abdomen. With each inhalation, let the sun's energy fill your solar plexus chakra.

- Imagine a yellow sunflower blossoming and opening over your solar plexus.

The
Heart
Chakra

6

Vedic name:	Anahata
Number:	The fourth chakra
Other names:	Green chakra
Central concept:	Love, relating, respect, creativity
Color:	Green
Lotus petals:	Twelve
Shapes:	Cross
Element:	Air
Planet:	Venus
Zodiac sign:	Libra
Health connection:	Heart, lungs, upper digestive tract
Balance:	Yin, feminine, negative
Gland:	Thymus
Sense:	Touch
Mantra:	Yam
Music:	Flute, woodwind instruments

Location

Unsurprisingly, the heart chakra is based in the center of the chest in the area of the heart. It is associated with the heart, lungs, thorax, upper digestive tract, and ribs.

Basic Purpose

The heart chakra is concerned with love and also with the ability to relate to others. It is also associated with the ability to love and respect ourselves, to be creative, and to be wise. This chakra is the gateway between the humanity-orientated lower chakras and the more divinely-orientated upper ones. The heart chakra is concerned with emotional security and with loving comfort. It seeks to form a balance between the need for love and for spiritual excellence, so it rules selflessness, compassion, devotion, and a sensible measure of sacrifice on behalf of others. The heart chakra concerns physical and emotional healing, but also creativity, artistry, music, and crafts. In a way, it is also connected to the ideas of those things that offer us fun, amusement, and uplift, in addition to relaxation, rest, and recovery.

A Strong Heart Chakra

This is the second of the *emotional* chakras, as opposed to the instinctual, mental, or spiritual ones. Obviously those with strong heart chakras are loving and unselfish, but they don't allow themselves to become martyrs or to be manipulated by others. These people don't flee from emotional commitment, because they are happy to love others, but they like to be loved in return. They don't need to play games. They forgive themselves when they do something wrong, and they understand and forgive others. Those with strong heart chakras neither hoard money nor spend it stupidly; they are neither stingy nor overly generous. They are balanced in every aspect of their lives. Those who have a strong heart chakra are reasonable to live with, work with, and to be around because they have a healthy self-respect, and they also gain the respect of others. Some of those with a strong heart chakra take a calculated decision to give up the chance of fun and freedom in order to take care of sick relatives, while others might even take up vocations in a religious order. Many choose to work with the needy.

One aspect of this chakra is the ability to cope when times are bad, which means that these individuals can handle loss, separation, bereavement, and heartache with a degree of equilibrium. They are not cold or unemotional, but they don't fall into a heap of self-pity or dejection when things go wrong. They have a measure of spiritual acceptance, and they know that even bad times are necessary for growth and understanding. These folk hope for the best, and they trust others unless they find a good reason not to.

Someone with a good heart chakra will often choose a career that involves working with people. They work in the public sector or in jobs that require teamwork and that help people in some way. They work with children, the elderly, the weak, the handicapped, or those who need advice, and if they don't happen to need money, they take up voluntary work.

There is a measure of self-acceptance and of self-knowledge, so this person knows that while he or she may not be perfect, he or she is pretty much all right.

Too Much Heart Chakra

These subjects can put the needs of others above their own to a great extent, perhaps by choosing a partner who is very needy or needs to be rescued from alcohol, drugs, gambling, or some other destructive habit. Misplaced loyalty is common.

At the worst end of the spectrum, these people can be manipulative and possessive or fond of making emotional scenes. Their love is conditional; it is only doled out when the other person does what they want, and they will withhold love when the other person needs it most. They can make a partner or child's life a complete misery. Sometimes the person is self-centered, possessive, and jealous, or power hungry, bitter, and prone to hatred. This subject finds it impossible to forgive.

Not Enough Heart Chakra

Just as an angry and confrontational person can drive others away, so can a whining, self-pitying, and dependent one. Both behaviors are a form of manipulation. Just as those with too much heart chakra can give too much of themselves to others, so can they if they don't have enough, because this is two sides of the same coin. Some people give far too much of themselves in the hope of obtaining or maintaining the approval of others.

In many ways, this chakra is about courage. All situations that involved relating to others, whether at home, at work, or elsewhere, require courage, common sense, and the ability to set limits. Thus, those who lack heart chakra energy may allow others to walk all over them. Alternatively, they might feel unlovable or unworthy of love. The individual might be stuck in a rut and lack the courage or energy to move out of it. Other problems might arise due to fear of the future. The person might be paralyzed by envy or they may feel unattractive, immobile, and helpless to effect change in their lives.

Interestingly, this individual may be perfectly happy, but just not be interested in romantic love or in relationships at all. He or she may get fulfillment in life through other routes—perhaps by creating a great garden, creating great art, looking after pets, or via some absorbing job or hobby.

Body and Health

Naturally, the heart is ruled by this chakra, but the heart chakra also rules the circulation, lungs, and rib cage. The heart chakra is associated with such ailments as asthma, allergies, and pneumonia, and it is also associated with problems in the upper spine and shoulders. The heart chakra is metaphorically linked to the air element, so it rules breathing difficulties. Those with a powerful heart chakra might cough or find it hard to breathe when they are upset or excited. This chakra also rules the immune system; therefore, it is associated with chronic fatigue syndrome, AIDS, Type I diabetes, and problems with cell growth. The heart chakra is also associated with the thymus and growth hormones, and it also rules the shoulders, arms, and breasts.

Spiritual Link

Tradition says that this chakra is associated with out-of-body experiences and astral travel. It also rules spiritual knowledge, so those who have a healthy heart chakra make wonderful counselors, healers, doctors, psychologists, and therapists. Some spiritual healers feel this chakra opening when they start to work.

Those who have a strong heart chakra can make excellent salespeople. They like and understand people, so they know instinctively how to make customers feel comfortable. This chakra can denote "putting one's heart" into things like charitable work or social work—any activity that is for the benefit of others.

Exercises for the Heart Chakra

Affirmation: I Give and Receive Love

- Visualize a green bud at your sternum. With each breath you inhale, the bud expands and unfolds its leaves, increasing the life force within this chakra.

- Get out into nature. Stand with your back against a tree, your shoulder blades making contact. Breathe in the energy of the tree, feeling it entering your back and entering your heart.

- Resist the urge to find fault in everything.

- Give a prayer of thanks every day for all you have.

The
Throat
Chakra

7

Vedic name:	Vishuddha
Number:	The fifth chakra
Other names:	Light blue chakra
Central concept:	Communication
Color:	Sky blue
Lotus petals:	Sixteen
Shapes:	Cup
Element:	Air/Ether
Planet:	Mercury
Zodiac sign:	Virgo
Health connection:	Throat
Balance:	Yang, masculine, positive
Gland:	Thyroid and Parathyroid
Sense:	Hearing
Facial area:	Throat
Mantra:	Ham
Music:	Singing

Location

The throat chakra runs through the neck from the lower part of the throat to the lower part of the cervical spine, more or less where it joins the shoulders. This chakra rules the thyroid and parathyroid, ears, mouth, and lower face. It also concerns the neck, the top of the shoulders, and the upper spine, along with the upper areas of the bronchial system. It is associated with speech and hearing.

Basic Purpose

This chakra rules communication and language. Apart from the obvious matter of being able to get a point across and argue a case, this chakra also symbolizes communication in the form of writing, poetry, music, and art. A less obvious form of communication is the ability to listen and to really *hear* what others are saying.

Some traditions say that the back part of this chakra (the back of the neck) relates to one's profession and one's place in society, while the front area concerns communication and hearing.

In a practical sense, the throat chakra controls growth and the development of the growth glands and growth hormones. In a metaphorical sense, it is also associated with the concept of growth of character through experience. Part of being an adult is the ability to take personal responsibility, so this is another attribute of a healthy throat chakra. On a more mundane level, which is nevertheless extremely important, it rules the ability to work and to earn money.

A Strong Throat Chakra

This is the first of the *mental* chakras, as opposed to the instinctual, emotional, or spiritual chakras, so it is associated with logic, reason, and common sense. People with strong throat chakras are loyal, calm, tactful, and trustworthy. They take responsibility for their own actions, they don't blame others for their own shortcomings, and neither do they blame others when things go wrong.

They exude authority. These people can see through lies and manipulation, and their instincts are good; because they enjoy argument and debate, they may be drawn to careers in legal work or politics. They take personal responsibility for their decisions, they set realistic goals, and they get things done. They succeed in the material world, and they live fulfilling lives. However, when things don't work out, they are able to accept what cannot be. They are realistic.

Those who have an abundant and healthy throat chakra are independent, so they rarely lean on others. Having said this, there is an instinctive knowledge that the universe or some higher power exists, so when they need help, they know that they can pray for it and receive it. There is an unconscious spiritual attitude to everything they do, so they are honest and decent and charitable toward others.

These people can be persuasive, so they negotiate well and they can be excellent salespeople. They can cope with accounting, budget and treasury work, business communications, and making deals that work for all the parties that are concerned. A strong throat chakra encourages individuals to stretch themselves, to accept challenges, and to aim high. These people can envision the future that they want, they can see where they want to be, and they can work backward from that point to create a strategy for achieving their aims. They are good at long-term planning, but they may be less able to deal with details than others are.

Too Much Throat Chakra

Those who have too much throat chakra express their opinions easily but they don't stop and listen to what others have to say. They may be prejudiced, rigid, and opinionated. They can't empathize with those who are different from them or those whose ideas and opinions are not like theirs.

At the worst end of the spectrum, these people can be intolerant. They blame others, and they refuse to take personal responsibility for things that go wrong. They may be talkative, arrogant, self-righteous, spiteful, and boring. They never express sympathy or feel empathy with others. At heart, these loud, bullying people are actually cowards who don't have the courage of their convictions.

They avoid work, or cherry pick the nice jobs and leave the boring or dirty jobs for others to do. They take credit for the ideas and achievements of others. At heart, they are jealous of others.

Not Enough Throat Chakra

These subjects are their own worst enemies, because they don't stand up for themselves or speak up when they feel an injustice. Sometimes they attract bullies into their lives, in the mistaken belief that the bully is a strong person who will protect them. Some weak throat chakra characters may lie to save the feelings of others or to protect themselves from someone else's anger.

They are dishonest with themselves, but they may feel that is the only way they can cope. They may live with impossible situations because they are afraid to speak up or walk out of a bad situation and face the uncertainty of a new one. Some accept too much blame and shame for things that are beyond their control.

At worst, they whine and they are pessimists who blame others for everything. They can be crafty or they may use manipulation to get their own way. They look backward and wallow in memories of the past. These subjects harbor grudges.

Body and Health

Naturally, the throat chakra is associated with the throat, but also the respiratory system and the vocal chords. This chakra rules colds, flu, coughs, asthma, allergies, ulcers, sore throats, tonsillitis, laryngitis, and so on. It rules the jaw, the teeth, and the start of the digestive system, which includes swallowing and reflux (hiatal hernia). It can be associated with eating disorders such as anorexia and bulimia. It also rules the thyroid and parathyroid glands, so it can relate to growth and development through its connection with growth hormones.

This chakra is associated with the ears, so it links with deafness and the organs of balance. When this chakra needs healing, chanting can help, as can listening to music, dancing, and moving rhythmically.

In women, it is linked to the menstrual cycle, PMS, menopause, mood swings, night sweats, fevers, and itches.

Spiritual Link

It is the spiritual aspect of this chakra that is the most important, because this chakra symbolizes the crossing point between the mundane world and the realm of spirit. The traditional task for the throat chakra is purification because it acts as a filter that traps whatever comes up from the earthy chakras before it can be drawn up into the heavenly ones that lie above. Remember that, even in the most basic kind of spiritual work, before you start you need to open your chakras and either bring light down from above or raise light and energy from below. Therefore, there is a need to protect the delicate heavenly chakras, and the throat chakra acts as a kind of gatekeeper. This might be the reason why so many people cough when opening their chakras.

Specifically, this chakra rules clairaudience, so a well-aligned throat chakra is an essential aid to those who have the rare gift of being able to *hear* spirit.

Exercises for the Throat Chakra

Affirmation: I Express

This chakra helps people to pray, chant, and to access the universe. We can help our throat chakra to do its work by using such techniques as drumming, humming, chanting mantras, singing hymns, sacred songs, or praying. This chakra allows people to pray for what they need and to tune in to their inner voice.

The
Brow
Chakra

8

Vedic name:	Ajna
Number:	The sixth chakra
Other names:	Third eye chakra, indigo chakra
Central concept:	Knowledge, clarity
Color:	Indigo blue
Lotus petals:	A circle with a petal on each side
Shapes:	Star of David
Element:	Light
Planet:	Jupiter
Zodiac sign:	Pisces
Health connection:	Head
Balance:	Yang, masculine, positive
Gland:	Pineal/pituitary
Sense:	Sight
Facial area:	Eyes, skull
Mantra:	AUM
Music:	Sacred songs and music

Location

This chakra is often called *the third eye*. Some say that it is located between the eyes, while others believe that it sits in the center of the forehead. Some sources say it rules the pineal gland, and others say it rules the pituitary gland.

Basic Purpose

This chakra is concerned with the connection to the spirit world, so it rules such things as extrasensory perception and the ability to contact or receive messages from "spirit." It is an essential part of channeling and spiritual healing.

On a mundane level, it rules self-knowledge and being able to take responsibility for one's own actions.

A Strong Brow Chakra

Now we are moving away from the day-to-day world and beginning to move toward the spiritual realms. Having said this, this chakra still has some connection to the mundane world, so it straddles the gulf between our world and the next, so to speak.

This chakra is concerned with *vision*, in the sense of receiving and being able to interpret clairvoyant visions and the information that comes in the form of dreams or in symbols. This chakra rules everything connected to "second sight" and to spirit messages. The brow chakra opens very quickly. If you try your hand at Tarot readings, it will open without any great effort, and if you watch

"Readers" working, you will often see them absent-mindedly rubbing their foreheads while doing so. This chakra is especially useful in visualization, meditation, and for those who have the gift of seeing auras. It is linked to remote viewing and intuition. It allows the subject to see through other people and to pick up on their real motives.

This sector rules thought, ideas, and inspiration, particularly ideas that one can actually bring to life. An example of this would be to write a play and then see it performed on the stage. There is a symbolic idea that connects to routes, roadways, and pathways here, so someone with a strong brow chakra can find a way through a dilemma or a route or pathway that leads from one situation to another.

The brow chakra is associated with memory, but it doesn't cling to the past or harbor bitterness about it because it rules the ability to learn from past hurts and to move on from them. In practical terms, a strong brow chakra endows people with decency, faithfulness, sympathy for others, clear sight, idealism, and integrity. It brings a reverence for all life and a responsible attitude to everything. Those who have strong brow chakras take responsibility for themselves and their actions, and they can also take care of those who need their strength.

People with strong brow chakras should pursue careers that have long-term goals, such as government, the insurance industry, money management, fund raising, civil engineering, or town planning. These people are visionaries, and have the courage to visualize something and make it happen.

Too Much Brow Chakra

Too much brow chakra is the sign of those who are badly behaved, who go on to ignore or excuse their own bad behavior, while at the same time judging others and finding them wanting. These individuals are obstinate, and their minds are stuck in a rut. They hide from the truth, and they can be bossy, domineering, insensitive, and full of superiority. They display little concern for others and they have even less contact with reality. They are totally into their own needs and desires.

A rather odd effect of an overpowering brow chakra is the concept of the spiritual bore. These people discover the world of mediums, ESP, ghosts, and so forth, and they become so immersed in it that they lose touch with reality and forget to use common sense. Like all bores, they have only one topic of conversation and a lack of balance.

In the worst of cases, their strong opinions can lead them to be racist or xenophobic.

Not Enough Brow Chakra

These subjects lack self-confidence and they are short of self-esteem. They are sensitive and easily hurt, so they suffer feelings of inadequacy. They can buy into and actually believe the opinions of those who enjoy putting them down. They over-analyze or over-rationalize situations, and they find it hard to move on after a put-down. Not unexpectedly, this might be a legacy of a poor childhood or the result of a past-life situation.

These people are intuitive but unfocused, so they don't achieve much, and they never manage to build up their self-confidence.

They sacrifice too much to others. They may put themselves last "for the sake of peace" or because they don't know how to stand up for themselves. There is a fine line between admiration and envy, and those with a poor brow chakra find themselves crossing it. Sometimes circumstances that are beyond their control lead to isolation and loneliness.

The ancient idea of this chakra is that it represents the quality of the relationship between the subject and the mother. Obviously, a good relationship is indicated if the chakra is strong but a poor relationship if the chakra is weak, and the mother might hurt, use, or manipulate the subject.

Body and Health

Problems with this chakra lead to headaches, migraine, neuralgia, sinusitis, dizziness, or even a fuzzy feeling due to fatigue and lack of sleep. Sleep can be disturbed due to menopause, so it is no surprise to find this chakra connected to those hormonal problems that cause hot flashes, sweating, and bloating.

The brow chakra rules the left eye, the pituitary, the central nervous system, the brain, and everything in the head, including tumors, strokes, blindness, and spinal difficulties. Needless to say, this chakra rules movement and coordination.

Spiritual Link

On a rather grand scale, the brow chakra is said to be one of the seats of the soul. It indicates the inner being and the source of creative energy. Some say it holds Akashic Records and our experiences of past lives. It is said to hold the key to the soul's purpose in this lifetime. The brow chakra encourages people to look into what might exist in the rest of the universe and find the reason for our existence.

On a more down to earth level, this chakra also relates to emotional intelligence and maturity, and it helps us to see what's behind our own actions and what's behind those of others. It brings the gifts of intuition and inspiration, and it allows us to access messages from the spirit world. It is especially connected to clairvoyance and second sight.

Exercises for the Brow Chakra

Affirmation: I See

- Focus your inner gaze at an indigo orb spinning between your eyebrows.

- Imagine your brow chakra as a balloon. As you breathe in, feel it growing with life force.

- Keep a dream journal.

- Enjoy creative arts and crafts.

- Go star-gazing.

The
Crown
Chakra

9

Vedic name:	Sahasrara
Number:	The seventh chakra
Other names:	Violet chakra
Central concept:	Spirituality
Color:	Violet, purple, white, or gold
Lotus petals:	1,000
Shapes:	Lotus, lily
Element:	Light
Planet:	Saturn
Zodiac sign:	Capricorn
Health connection:	Head and central nervous system
Balance:	Ying/Yang, masculine and feminine
Gland:	Pineal/pituitary
Sense:	Oneness with the universe
Facial area:	Head
Mantra:	NNN
Music:	Silence

Location

This chakra is located at the top of the head, slightly to the back of it. Interestingly, when a child is baptized, the priest closes the chakra with holy water. Jews, Muslims, and Catholic officials such as Cardinals and Popes wear caps over this chakra. Ancient tradition says that wearing a head covering allows you to focus energy on your third eye, the brow chakra, and provides a sense of containment during spiritual practice. It literally helps "keep your head together."

Basic Purpose

This chakra is hard to define, and it is all too easy to descend into pseudo-spiritual babble while attempting to do so—but I will do my best to keep things simple and straightforward.

Consider the idea of connectedness and you are well on the way to understanding this chakra. For instance, it links all of us to everyone else on earth so it suggests the idea of "the brotherhood of man." It unites us with heaven, the universe, and with spirit, but it also reaches down through the chakra system to connect us to the earth beneath our feet. Therefore, it rules the *interconnectedness* of everything. The crown chakra symbolizes faith and trust, along with the ability to pray and to know that the Divine will lead us in the right direction.

A person with a strong crown chakra looks forward to the future with optimism, and the chakra is also associated with joy, happiness, and peace of mind.

A Strong Crown Chakra

People with a strong crown chakra are idealistic and have a deep reverence for all forms of life. They are kind hearted and may be somewhat self-sacrificing. They can empathize with others to the extent that they almost feel their pain. They understand all manner of people. They are highly intelligent.

This chakra contains memories of the past and of past lives but also some inkling of heaven and the next life. This is the gateway to the higher consciousness, to spirituality, guided intuition, and an understanding of the real meaning of life and of the afterlife. Those who have a strong crown chakra understand their purpose on earth and can see their best way forward. However, their values are spiritual rather than material, and so the path they choose to follow is spiritual rather than material as well. They are not members of the rat race. The crown chakra rules faith, trust, prayer, meditation, and wisdom. It also links to happiness, bliss, and moments of true ecstasy and joy. It brings a sense of balance and spiritual awareness.

Oddly enough, feelings of loneliness, isolation, bereavement, and absolute desolation can be linked to this chakra even when it is strong. The concept is not easy to grasp, but the idea is that when people are utterly lost, bereaved, betrayed, or unhappy, they are most likely to turn to prayer. It is at these times that they ask questions such as; "Why me, why this, why now?" It is then that they pray for the strength to cope with life. Misery turns people inward to contemplate the spiritual side of life, and this chakra is all about such inward journeys. Thus, in a strange way, awareness and growth of character can come out of heartbreak.

On a mundane level, those who have an abundance of strength in this chakra might choose to live in an environment where they don't need to earn a living, such as becoming a rabbi, nun, priest, social worker, or perhaps an overseas aid worker. Having said that, there is nothing written anywhere that says this chakra is against someone earning money, but they should also possess a good soul. Indeed, those who work, earn money, and pay their bills have a sense of responsibility that denotes a strong crown chakra, but they never view money as the prime motive for doing anything.

These people are ethical and they always try to do a good day's work in exchange for a good day's pay. If they sell something or perform a service, they will be happy doing so if they believe that the product or service is of real benefit to others. These individuals can't stand advantage-takers, swindlers, and liars. They are honest and decent themselves, and they prefer to keep company with others who are equally honest and decent.

Tradition suggests that the crown chakra carries memories of a father's love, along with feelings of sadness at having to grow up and leave him.

Too Much Crown Chakra

This belongs to those who are too involved with the world of spirit to be able to function in the real world. They need to become grounded. They may pray all the time. They take themselves very seriously, and they may be religious bores who have no ordinary interests and no other topics of conversation. They may have a judgmental and "holier than thou" attitude that makes others feel uncomfortable, and they consider themselves superior to those around them.

Not Enough Crown Chakra

Individuals with a weak crown chakra are full of fears and phobias, so much so that they cannot enjoy life or look forward to the future with optimism. They fear death. If their lives are difficult, they find it hard to make change or improve their situation or move on. They have no faith in God or faith in the future, so they often feel blocked and unable to progress. They cannot pray, and they don't even try to access their own higher consciousness.

At worst, those who are lacking in crown chakra energy might be money-minded, mundane, and earthly. At best, they may be wonderful money makers and they probably value other people by measuring the money or possessions that they have. They may be completely caught up with the idea of wealth and possessions, and become materially rich but lack compassion or soul.

Often it takes loss, heartbreak, or bereavement for ordinary people to consider the soul, karma, the afterlife, and their purpose on earth, which is why severe distress is often the start of spiritual development.

An overly weak crown chakra is allied to a poor father/child relationship, where either the father is a bad parent or the subject is bad to his or her father.

Body and Health

The crown chakra rules the brain, especially the right side of it, and it is also associated with the central nervous system. Thus, there may be such problems as multiple sclerosis, schizophrenia, hallucinations, Parkinson's disease, epilepsy, Alzheimer's disease, bipolar disorder, or some other kind of severe mental disorder. This chakra also rules clinical depression.

Tradition suggests that the crown chakra rules the right eye, varicose veins, and the skin. Thus, it is associated with rashes, eczema, warts, moles, bacteria, and probably also skin cancer.

Spiritual Link

Those who have a strong crown chakra are aware of the oneness and harmony with the universe and with all humankind. They are kind, gentle, and generous. They can see something good in the most difficult of people and they have time for even the most unsavory or unwanted members of society. Needless to say, wealth and money don't attract them. Piling up wealth in heaven is more their style.

This chakra is the gateway to the spiritual world. Tradition says that the soul leaves the body via this chakra

Exercises for the Crown Chakra

Affirmation: I Know

- Envision a violet orb spinning above the top of your head, opening and allowing white light to enter. Feel Divine Light spiralling down through your body.

- Listen to everything and read everything. Keep your mind open.

- Practicing meditation is the best exercise for this chakra.

Part Three

CHAKRA
HEALING

Healing
Physical
Ailments

10

Blockages and imbalances in your chakra system can result in disturbances in your physical and mental health. Chakras affect every aspect of your well-being, from emotions, mind, spirit, to life itself. By understanding what each chakra does—which body/mind system it governs—you can become more involved in healing yourself and others, as well as simply maintaining your good health.

If you are unwell, please go to a conventional medical practitioner, and visit your dentist, optician, podiatrist, or other relevant professional, as required. Having said this, complementary therapies are ideal for some chronic ailments where conventional medicine can do little to help, and the same goes for some stress-related ailments. Other ailments need conventional medicine or even counseling and psychotherapy, but the process may be speeded up or made easier by the use of complementary therapies or by spiritual healing. Many nonconventional therapies are now becoming mainstream—at one time osteopathy, chiropractic, aromatherapy, acupuncture, hypnotherapy, and reflexology were all considered "out there." I've seen some brow chakra ailments respond well to cranial-sacral osteopathy or zero balancing, which is a gentle form of massage and muscular manipulation.

If you are receiving conventional medical treatment, please remember to tell your doctor about any complementary treatment that you are also having, especially those that put things into the body, such as homeopathy, herbal treatments, or aromatherapy.

If you are providing healing or performing a chakra therapy, you don't really need to make an effort to open your chakras, as they tend to open automatically as soon as you start work.

Here is a review of the seven chakras and the body functions they govern:

- Base Chakra: legs, base of body, adrenal system

- Sacral Chakra: reproductive system, ovaries, testes

- Solar Plexus Chakra: digestion, pancreas, endocrine system

- Heart Chakra: heart, lungs, upper digestive tract

- Throat Chakra: throat ailments, and thyroid and parathyroid issues

- Brow Chakra: head and pineal/pituitary system

- Crown Chakra: head and central nervous system

Color Healing

Let us assume that you are a bit off color and you feel that a boost to one of your chakras would make you feel better. Try this very simple and noninvasive method for rebalancing a slightly wonky chakra. Take a piece of cloth or paper in the relevant chakra color and focus on the color. Breathe regularly and deeply for a while, as if you were taking the color into your body with each intake of breath.

Another simple and very pleasant form of chakra alignment is to add some fruits and vegetables of the appropriate color into your diet for a day or two. Don't just live on that one kind of food and exclude others, just make sure that you include one item of its kind in your diet each day. Unbalanced eating can make you ill. For instance, if you eat too much citrus fruit or fruit juice, you will end up with cystitis and headaches, while too many carrots will turn your skin yellow! Here are some chakra-based suggestions:

- Base: tomatoes, red plums, strawberries, and raspberries

- Sacral: oranges, carrots, apricots, and orange peppers

- Solar Plexus: bananas, parsnips, yellow peppers, lemons, and sweet corn

- Heart: green vegetables, apples, pears, gooseberries, and kiwi fruit

- Throat: plums, passion fruit, red grapes, blueberries

- Brow: blueberries, blackberries, and black currents

- Crown: radishes, blackberries, black olives

It might seem strange to use color for healing but it can have dramatic effects. About five or six hundred years ago, if a child became infected with chicken pox, the parents would give the child "the red treatment." This meant temporarily replacing the curtains and bedclothes in the child's room with ones made out of red material. This weird therapy works, because something in the spectrum of the red color prevents chicken pox from forming scars. Similarly, bad cases of psoriasis can be treated by ultraviolet light, and some forms of psoriasis improve when exposed to the ultraviolet rays in sunlight.

Using color is especially beneficial when used to change one's mood. When I am due to give a talk or a presentation, I instinctively choose to wear bright colors to give me confidence. If I need to be quiet and calm, I wear pale shades of blue, lavender, or a neutral shade of cream. If you have trouble sleeping or relaxing, you should decorate your bedrooms and sitting rooms in cool, quiet, pastel shades. If your child finds it hard to sleep, decorate his or her room in soft and neutral colors. People love to decorate children's rooms in very bright primary colors with cartoon type figures and patterns, and then they wonder why the poor kids can't sleep!

Altar Healing

There are forms of healing that are noninvasive but very effective in their way, and here we can take ideas that come from religion as a whole and Wicca in particular. The following suggestions might help ease physical ailments, but they are particularly useful when helping someone who is unhappy or ill at ease.

Find a quiet spot in your house and put a small table in it. If you are short of space, a bookshelf or the top of a chest of drawers will do. Put a clean white cloth and a candle holder on your altar. Select the color that is appropriate to the chakra that you wish to heal, then get a piece of cloth or a paper napkin in that color and place it on the altar. You can also use gems and stones of the appropriate type for a certain chakra. Add a candle or tea light in the relevant color. You might like to put a little dish with some appropriate essential oil on the altar or use an oil burner, or use a joss stick (incense stick) with an aroma that feels right for that chakra. You can put ribbons, buttons, beads, or anything else on the altar that you like and that happen to be the appropriate color.

(**Note**: If you light candles or joss sticks, please stay in the room and keep an eye on them. Don't put candles, joss sticks, or burners in a drafty area where they might fall over and cause a fire.)

If you are giving healing to yourself, put your photograph on the altar, and if you are giving healing to someone else, use his or her photo. If you have a particular piece of jewelry or other item that means a lot to you, you can add that, along with anything else that might be appropriate to you. The same goes for things that are appropriate to your friend or to the things that relate to the ailment or the problem. This might be a letter about a hospital appointment, a piece of work from an upcoming exam, or anything else that represents the person or situation that needs help. Even writing the worry or problem down on a piece of paper and putting that on the altar will help. Once again, I remind you never to leave lighted candles, burners, or incense sticks unattended.

Gemstones and Metals

A very nice form of energy healing is to use gems and other materials directly on the chakras. For this, you need to have your patient lie down (either belly up or belly down) and then place stones or pieces of metal on the various chakras, as this will boost the healing energy. Where the base chakra is concerned, you might prefer to place it on the person's legs, just above the knees rather than in the traditional base chakra position. The choice of stones and metals is pretty large and opinions vary as to which should be used where, as some are assigned to more than one chakra. As always, do what feels right to you.

Cleansing and Energizing

Before you use any crystals, stones, metals, or other items, you should take the following steps:

- Collect some rainwater and wash the stones in it. Leave them to dry outside in the sunlight or on a sunny windowsill.

- Lay the stones on a clean cloth and imagine white light coming down on them from the universe, and ask for the stones to help those who are in need of healing or of relief from mental stress.

- Then put them in a nice bag or box and keep them out of harm's way until you want to use them.

The Chinese believe that all objects that are used for spiritual purposes should be kept on a shelf above head height, in order to keep them closer to heaven.

Which Crystals to Use on Which Chakra

The following lists show some of the stones or metals that you might like to choose as a healing boost for each chakra.

Base Chakra

Black onyx

Garnet

Hematite

Jasper

Pyrite

Ruby

Obsidian

Flint

Iron

Sacral Chakra

Amber

Aventurine

Carnelian

Citrine

Tiger's eye

Coral

Jasper

Moonstone

Fire opal

Topaz

Silver

Solar Plexus Chakra

- Amber
- Amethyst
- Calcite
- Citrine
- Sodalite
- Tiger's eye
- Topaz
- Gold

Heart Chakra

- Aventurine
- Emerald
- Jade
- Chrysocolla
- Agate
- Peridot
- Rose quartz
- Malachite
- Moonstone
- Pink tourmaline
- Green tourmaline
- Copper

Throat Chakra

Turquoise

Aquamarine

Lapis lazuli

Blue lace agate

Sodalite

Amazonite

Celestine

Fluorite

Sapphire

Cinnabar

Brow Chakra

Clear quartz

Lapis lazuli

Amethyst

Azurite

Calcite

Sapphire

Fluorite

Tin

Crown Chakra

> Diamond
>
> Zircon
>
> Amethyst
>
> Pearl
>
> Clear quartz
>
> Rose quartz
>
> Lead

Essential Oils

It is always advisable to consult a qualified aromatherapist for the best treatment, because oils can have a profound effect on the body. It is probably better not to use these on the skin if someone is seriously ill or if they are taking other medication. There are special burners that you can use with essential oils that will disperse the essence around the room, which is better than putting it directly on the skin. Please ask a qualified person to show you how to safely use the burner rather than experimenting with it. If you understand the principles of aromatherapy and can safely use oils on your own or your client's skin, always dilute the oil with a suitable carrier oil.

Base Chakra

Oak Moss

Patchouli

Vetiver

Sacral Chakra

Clary sage

Jasmine

Cinnamon

Rose

Citrus

Solar Plexus Chakra

Bergamot

Geranium

Ginger

Grapefruit

Juniper

Lemon

Peppermint

Rosemary

Heart Chakra

Bergamot

Rose

Ylang ylang

Lemongrass

Throat Chakra

Rosemary

Chamomile

Frankincense

Sandalwood

Geranium

Brow Chakra

Lavender

Hyacinth

Geranium

Pine

Sage

Rose

Crown Chakra

Frankincense

Myrrh

Sandalwood

Bay

Lavender

Valerian

Jasmine

Emotional and Mental Ailments

11

There are thousands of emotional and psychological situations that plague us, but we can only focus on a few obvious ones in this book. Let us look at some scenarios that typify the problems attached to each chakra and see what sensible steps you can take to help yourself.

Our emotional and mental states are generally the driving forces behind our actions. The first step is to recognize and change your behavior; this will have a strengthening and balancing effect on the chakra that governs each emotional situation.

Also, refer back to the lists of gemstones and essential oils in the last chapter and carry those correspondences forward to the chakras discussed in this chapter. For example, if you are frequently in a state of stress over your day-to-day survival—even if this is just your ability to cope—this is a base chakra issue. Try wearing a patchouli scent or a garnet pendent.

Base Chakra

The base chakra is about survival, so at the most fundamental level, this means having enough clean water, food, clothing, shelter, and appropriate medicines to stay alive and healthy. A comparison would be to look at your own life with all its ups and downs, and compare it to that of someone who is stuck in a refugee camp in Africa, or someone wandering around in a state of shock following some natural disaster. In more mundane terms, it is wise to avoid back alleys, dangerous areas, and shortcuts or to take part in improperly supervised extreme sports. In emotional terms, being on the receiving end of sustained bullying is no good for your mental health.

Where physical or mental danger is concerned, your best bet is to sort things out quickly, even if it means moving away from a particular area or dumping harmful friends and relatives. If you are at a social event and someone bothers you, make a bathroom visit and while there, call a cab and go home. Do this even if you have a partner or friends at the event, just tell them you have a migraine and sort out the real reason for your departure later if you even feel that's necessary. Never accept a ride home from a creepy person.

Give yourself spiritual sustenance by doing the things that make you happy, such as singing, dancing, swimming, playing sports, and having fun. Sports, energetic activities, and dancing are particularly attuned to the base chakra. Alternatively, calm the chakra down by meditating and daydreaming. When you have some time to yourself, sit or lay down, close your eyes, and imagine white light that is flecked with healing turquoise or pale blue coming down and flooding your body. Let this light focus most of its energy on the base chakra.

Realize your limitations and forgive yourself when you discover that you can't do everything to perfection. Take a rest from time to time

Sacral Chakra

The sacral chakra rules relationships and everything that can happen within them. This chakra rules gut feelings, and yours will tell you the truth if you listen to them with honesty, so listen to your inner voice and trust your own instincts. Filter everything through your own intellect. Don't allow yourself to be railroaded into anything, whether it is sex, giving money or support to someone, or allowing them to "crash" in your home. Don't turn your back on your friends and family just because you have found your soul mate. If your lover becomes jealous of the time you spend with friends and family, this is a warning sign of potential future abuse. Remind yourself that you can't possibly be responsible for everything that goes wrong in your life. You don't have enough power for that. Unpleasant things happen to all of us from time to time. It's just the way things are.

Solar Plexus Chakra

The solar plexus chakra rules self-esteem, self-respect, and personal power. Others might push you around or you might behave in a controlling or bullying manner to others. Aim for a happy medium where you don't shrink from the challenges of life but where you don't hurt others either. Look after your diet and health, take some exercise, drink plenty of water, and eat properly. This will make you feel better, so that you become strong enough to fight off moments of despair. If people take advantage of you, practice standing in front of a mirror and saying "no." Walk around your house or garden with your hand in a "stop" position and say, "Don't you dare take advantage of me!" If you can do this in a safe situation, you might just be able to do it when you need to.

If you are jealous of those who have money, status, or a better lifestyle than you, try envying the Queen of England because she has everything, and that will save you the bother of having to envy everyone between your level and hers. If you feel jealous of love rivals or if you yearn for someone who doesn't love you, use a meditation to envision some way of cutting yourself off from the painful situation or letting one go. Then take yourself off to fresh woods and pastures new. You may find new friends who appreciate you when you are in a new environment.

There are many meditations for getting rid of things. Try this one for example: Sit down quietly and open your chakras. Imagine a large plastic sack and see yourself holding the handles of the sack. Imagine the other person, the problem, or your feelings about the situation going into the sack. When the sack is full, then tie it up, put it into the garbage can, and then imagine yourself cutting the handles or letting them go. Wave the sack of trouble goodbye.

Heart Chakra

The heart chakra concerns love and relationships. Love makes the world go wrong! Love, self-sacrifice, and affection are wonderful and it is great to be kind, loving, and a giver, but not if you constantly choose unkind, unloving takers as partners. On the other hand, you may be too choosy and demanding for anyone to be able to stand your company for long. There are many courses that teach awareness, so why not take a few of them? Learn how to respect yourself and love yourself because then you will attract the respect and love of others.

If a love relationship starts well and then changes into something untenable, then accept that you might have to call it a day.

If you lie to yourself or to others or if you are constantly lied to, work out what's going on. For instance, is this just a case of a few little white lies that are designed to save unnecessary friction, or ask yourself whether you are frightened of your partner? Be honest with yourself.

Throat Chakra

The throat chakra is the chakra of communication—or the lack of it! My friend Lynne runs chakra workshops, and she says *this* is the chakra that most people have trouble with, and it is often the one with the greatest need for healing.

This chakra is associated with a host of communication problems, such as not speaking up when something bothers you or not letting others know how you really feel. Alternatively, you might be too quick to express unpleasant opinions or inclined to come out with remarks that you instantly regret. You may fuss about unimportant matters, or you may never say what you really mean. These are just a few of the many problems people have in communicating their own needs and feelings.

The other biggie is not listening to others. Once again, it might be worth taking courses that help you to understand yourself and others, but listening to what others have to say is a good way forward—albeit a very hard way at times.

Brow Chakra

The brow chakra rules excellence in behavior, faithfulness, courage, and truthfulness. It rules confidence in one's abilities, a realistic sense of one's own value, and a sense of purpose. Chakra treatment to this area can help people to become more able and more confident. It can also aid the development of intuition, sensitivity, and ability to channel or link to spirit.

Crown Chakra

The crown chakra rules the link to spirit and the first slight glimmering of the next world. This will need healing if the person is too interested in religion and spiritual matters for common sense to apply.

Other Chakras

As you will soon see, there are many other chakras, and if one happens to connect with a body area that is sore—such as a sore hand or knee—some healing directed into it can do no harm.

Part Four

ADDITIONAL CHAKRAS

Beyond the Seven Chakras

12

As I mentioned earlier in this book, tradition states that there are 78,000 chakras in the human body. Although not everybody agrees about the number or where they are situated, this list is commonly agreed upon by most people:

- Seven major chakras

- Twenty-one minor chakras

- Forty-nine tiny chakras

- The remainder are minute nano-chakras

When it comes to the extra chakras, there are a lot to choose from and many different ideas as to what they might be used for. Some are well known, but others are still subject to ongoing discussion among spiritual people.

Chart Your Chakras

Here is an easy way of keeping a record of the chakras in your own body. Find or take a photograph of yourself in full length—standing up, facing front, and wearing fitted clothes such as jeans and a T-shirt. A photo of yourself in a bathing suit would be even more accurate. Make a few photocopies, and use these to chart the chakras as you discover them. First circle the locations of the seven major chakras. Then be sensitive to other energy centers you experience in your body. It could be a hand, your elbow, your neck. Mark these down on your photo chart as well, perhaps circling them in a different color. When you have found all the chakras you want to use, make a nice tidy copy, mark in colors

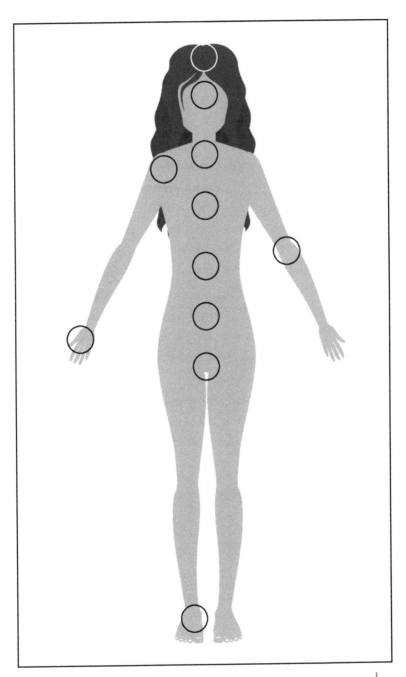

that you think are suitable, and then laminate the final picture. My feeling is that, over time, you will become aware of another six or eight chakras in addition to the basic seven.

Awareness can come through reading books, finding information on the Internet, or talking to healers and psychics, but it can also come through use and common sense. For example, you might suddenly realize that you habitually rub or scratch a particular part of your body when you are doing spiritual work. You may rub some other area when you are agitated or some other part of the body when you are particularly happy, and yet another area will bother you when you are thinking deeply.

Often there are chakras on either side of the body that mirror each other. For example, there are two on either side of the spine, below the shoulder blade, and these are linked to higher learning. If you want to put your mind to something deep or difficult, it might be worth focusing your mind on them for a moment or two, so that they open up for you.

Similarly, if you want to feel more confident, focus your mind on the chakras on either side of your pelvic area. Give them a surreptitious rub if it is convenient to do so.

The Hands and Arms

Every healer and many other psychics are aware that each hand has a chakra that runs right through it from the back of the hand to the palm.

These chakras are useful when giving healing, or when you wish to feel someone's or something's aura, or when you want to give a massage. They will help with anything that you need to do with your hands—even for something as ordinary as hairdressing! If you want to feel these chakras at work, try this exercise:

- Put your hands together in front of you.

- Part your hands to about eighteen inches.

- Slowly bring them back together.

- Stop when you feel a slight pressure; this feels as if the air between your hands has become thicker.

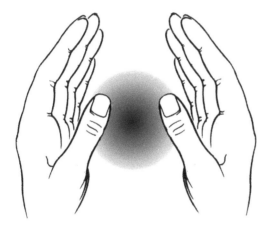

If nothing happens, try this. Hold your hands out in front of you with one palm facing upward and the other downward with a gap of about three or four inches between then. Then swap them around so that you change the hands that are facing up and down. Keep on swapping them until your arms feel tired. If you don't get much of a reaction from your own body alone, try this with someone else so that each of you has a palm that faces the other.

Fingers

Each fingertip has a little chakra of its own. If you want to see these in action, take a pendulum or use a pendant on a chain and hold this over your fingers one at a time. The pendulum will revolve in a different direction over each finger. If you don't get any reaction, try working on someone else's hands, because the interaction between you might make it work more successfully than doing it on yourself alone.

In practical terms, these chakras also help when giving healing or any kind of hands-on treatment.

Foot Chakras

Foot chakras go through the insteps and out through the soles of the feet. They correspond to each of the seven main chakras.

The foot chakras help you to ground yourself, so if you have been doing too much meditation or psychic or spiritual work and you feel light headed and spacey, or if you have a headache, try to get out of doors and stand or walk on the earth or on grass with bare feet for a few moments. Be careful not to cut or hurt your feet. These chakras link you to "Mother Earth" and help you to regain a sense of proportion. You might even like to extend some imaginary light from your body, down through your feet to the earth below. This is a calming exercise.

The foot chakras

Elbow Chakras

The elbows have chakras, but opinion varies as to whether these are shining out on the points of the elbows or going through them from side to side like a rivet.

Shoulder Chakras

These chakras run through the outer part of the shoulders, from front to back.

I feel my shoulder chakras opening whenever I do anything of a psychic or spiritual nature. Some books on chakras show the shoulder chakras as being in the armpit area; others show them running through the shoulders from the back of the body to the front, just below the area where a shoulder pad in a coat would sit.

The Eighth Chakra

The eighth chakra sits above the head and it is often depicted as a white glow or a white flower. I think this is where the confusion surrounding the color of the crown chakra arises. Some feel that it should be colored purple and others say white. My view is that the crown chakra is purple but that the eighth chakra that sits *above* the crown chakra is white.

Tradition says that at the time of death, the soul leaves the body through a small hole in the top of the head, and that the eighth chakra is the last link between the human world and all our bodily concerns; this chakra is the first link with world of spirit. It contains karmic residue that is taken into the first stages of the afterlife.

Not everyone agrees with this image, because many psychics report the spiritual body parting the physical one via an umbilical cord.

The Higher Chakras

Hindu tradition suggests that the eighth chakra is topped by another three chakras that line up above the head, with the last one being situated about two feet above the head. It is said that each of these has a different spiritual purpose:

9th chakra: Seat of the soul

10th chakra: Mind over matter

11th chakra: Universal unity

The higher chakras

Doubled Chakras

Here we return to the seven major chakras, but we now take a closer look at two of them. The doubled chakras are the heart chakra and the brow chakra. Some Hindu illustrations show these as one slightly above the other.

Doubled Heart Chakra

The twelve-petalled heart chakra, Anahata, deals with love. Directly below Anahata is a minor heart chakra known as Hrit, with eight petals. Within this second heart chakra is kalpu taru, the wish-fulfilling tree. It is said to symbolize the desire of what one wants in the world. As such, this second heart chakra rules earthly, romantic love, and the love of a child or of a family member or a friend or even a pet. This chakra can even be associated with obsessive love, although that is also strongly influenced by the base and sacral chakras.

The upper heart chakra is aligned to the love of God.

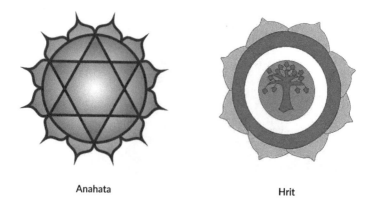

Anahata

Hrit

Doubled Brow Chakra

The double-petalled brow chakra, Ajna, is in the middle of the forehead and it is linked to mercy, gentleness, and empathy. It is the eye of intuition and intellect. Directly above the brow chakra is a minor chakra called Manas. Its function is to send perceptions from the five senses upward to the higher chakras. Manas has six petals, one for each of the five senses, and a sixth petal for what is perceived during sleep.

Kundalini

13

Kundalini is a powerful force or energy that rises up through the chakra system from base to crown. You can raise power and energy of kundalini through the chakra system to connect with universe or to link with a god or a particular deity or for specific forms of psychic work.

In the first chapter, I introduced the concept of prana, the vital life force that flows through the chakras. So how is kundalini different than prana? Kundalini is prana that has been curled up at the base of the spine (your base chakra) and when the kundalini force is awakened, this coiled prana is awakened and released with force, rising through all seven chakras in what is called *sushumna*. This rush of kundalini can take us ultimately to enlightenment. Kundalini is still part of the body's one prana, just a different manifestation.

Traditional illustrations depict kundalini as a snake that snoozes at the base of the body until something wakes it up, upon which it uncurls and rises up through the chakra system.

I have saved this chapter until last because it is important that your chakras are clear and balanced to allow kundalini to rise. Can you imagine a sudden, powerful surge blasting through your garden hose—only to discover you have a leaky hose? What a mess! And the kundalini will not arrive at its final destination.

I prefer to think of kundalini as white smoke rising upward from a fire and passing by the revolving drums of the chakras than as a snake uncurling. Perhaps it is just that our culture is not too keen on snakes, or maybe I object to the idea of my body being inhabited by one.

Kundalini is said to be the force that links us to the earth beneath our feet and the heavens above our heads. It brings sudden enlightenment and it can bring feelings of ecstasy of the kind that people experience when performing certain shamanic rituals. It can be activated by doing yoga and by meditating, and of course by opening the chakras and focusing on it.

Another way of raising kundalini is by having sex. When one experiences an especially powerful orgasm, it is not uncommon to see colors swirling around in your head for a few moments afterward, and this is part of the kundalini effect. When too much kundalini rushes to the head, or when it arrives there too quickly, you can feel spacey or you can get a headache. Have you ever developed a nasty headache after sex? If so, it is the kundalini force that is responsible. The way to ease this effect is to open the crown chakra so that the kundalini force is let free to reach the heavens.

Conclusion

So now we have taken a look at the chakra system, explored the seven major chakras in detail, and looked briefly into some others. We have discovered some ways of healing the emotional, mental, physical, and spiritual problems that arise when chakras are blocked, misaligned, or too open. You can ease these problems with energy healing, crystal healing, and by using appropriate complementary therapies, along with conventional medicine when it is needed. We have looked into some strange ideas, and we have explored the wonders of kundalini.

Now it is time for you to use your chakras in any way that you care to, but remember to shut them again after doing any heavy spiritual work, or you will feel invaded by unwanted energies and you will find it hard to sleep.

Good luck!

About the Author

Sasha Fenton has written well over one hundred books, and is well known for her clear, friendly style and her ability to make highly technical subjects easy to understand. She has had a life-long interest in esoteric studies, particularly palmistry, astrology, tarot, and divination systems. Her many books include *Body Reading Plain & Simple*, *Fortune Telling by Tarot Cards*, *Palmistry Plain & Simple*, *Fortune Teller's Handbook*, and *Secrets of Chinese Divination*.

In the early 1980s, Sasha joined the British Astrological and Psychic Society (BAPS), later becoming secretary and subsequently president of the society; she also spent some years on the British Advisory Panel on Astrological Education. Right from the start, Sasha wrote articles for *Mercury*, the BAPS quarterly magazine, and she still does from time to time. Sasha has written numerous articles for newspapers and magazines, including every major newspaper in Britain.

Other Titles in the *Plain & Simple* Series